Cooking is an art when you do it from your HEART

Maria Elena Congedo

From
mom
to
daughter

THE QUICK TIPS
OF ITALIAN COOKING

CONGEDO PUBLISHING

In Italy, love passes through food.
And I have always felt my mother impart it this way.
Every day. Through the smells, the tastes, the colors, the textures, the sounds of our kitchen.
Since, on tiptoe, I watched what was being kneaded on the marble table and I saw those skilled hands make the ingredients magically take shape.
When, as a teenager, I found it relaxing and festive to prepare with her the Sunday dessert.
When, at a university far from home, I received one of her famous packages of wonders, magical boxes capable of containing every delight of creation, especially prepared for me. And now, as a young woman who replicates her recipes in my daily life, or when in our country home in Southern Italy, I finally find the pulse of time marked by the choice of ingredients, setting the table, the liturgy of preparing meals. And I try to pass that on to little Rebecca. My mother taught me that cooking is an act of love. That at the table all of the feelings are conveyed: friendship, respect, joy, pain. Because the kitchen is the heart of the house and a plate has in it the essence of who prepared it. Their experience, imagination, sensitivity. Italy has strong and true flavors.

With thousands of facets, thousands of peculiarities. Talking with the food, communicating through the dishes, is an art, a tradition, an instinct. But every family, in Italy, has "its" cuisine, made of small and big secrets, savvy and rituals, tricks of the trade acquired by generations of testing, putting food on the table, of new elements gradually introduced and tested. It is a heritage that only a mother, not a mother-in-law, passes to her daughter and granddaughter! Because cooking is not just simply following a recipe. It is living and rejoicing, represented in a flavor, a taste, a smell. Cooking is to surrender oneself to others. To their palate, their judgment, their "belly". An Italian dish is a code, an atmosphere, a world. And so, to my mother, bestselling author of cookbooks like "Odori, colori e sapori della cucina Salentina", "Signori a Tavola", "Country chic kitchens" and "Puglia, ricette e sapori", after many years of far and "near" kitchen life, in which a lot of love is given and received, I dedicate this book that collects all her secrets and hands them on to my little Rebecca.

Maria Elena Congedo

CONTENTS

MEMO:

The antipasto should whet your appetite and not suppress it.

appetizers

BRESAOLA (DRIED BEEF) AND CREAM CHEESE ROLLS

INGREDIENTS
4 oz of thinly sliced bresaola
8 oz of cream cheese
chives
green salad

On each slice of bresaola, lay a teaspoon of cream cheese. Roll to close or bundle and tie with a chive, or hold it with a toothpick. Place the rolls on a bed of green salad and serve.

13

BRUSCHETTA
WITH TOMATO

INGREDIENTS
1 pound of bread (baguette is better)
7-8 large, firm and ripe tomatoes
2 cloves of garlic
1 bunch arugula or 12-15 basil leaves
Extra virgin olive oil and salt to taste

Cut the bread into slices. Toast them in the oven or toaster. Meanwhile, cut the tomatoes into small cubes, and place them in a bowl. Season with salt and oil. Wash and chop the arugula, set aside for final garnish. Do the same if you prefer basil. Rub each slice of bread with the garlic. Place the slices on a serving plate. With a spoon, spread the tomatoes on the toasted bread and add the arugula or basil to serve.

17

18

STEP 1

STEP 3

STEP 2

21

CHEESE DUMPLINGS

INGREDIENTS
1 pound of puff pastry
$^1/_2$ pound of sweet provola or fresh soft cheese

Roll out the pastry to a thickness of $^1/_4$ inches.
Cut into squares with sides 4 inches long
(make some more from the end scraps). Dice
the cheese. Place a couple of cubes of cheese at
the center of the squares of dough. Close the
bundle. Seal the edges. Bake in preheated oven
at 350° until the pastry is golden.

STEP 1

STEP 2

24

STEP 3

STEP 4

25

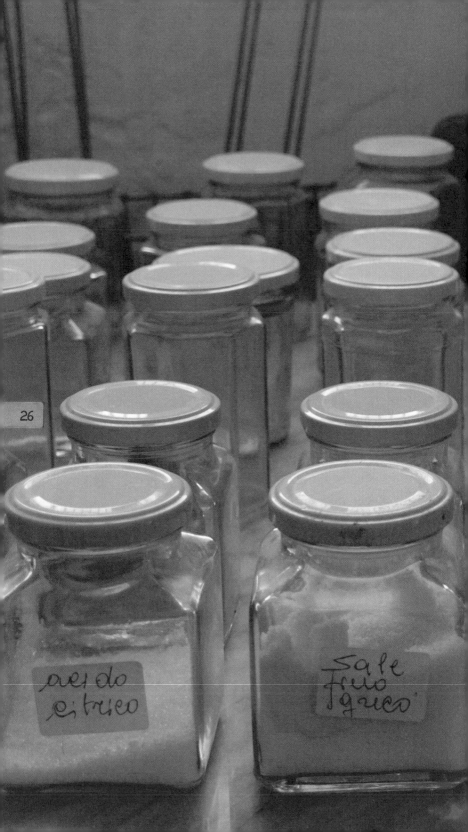

CRACKERS WITH MASCARPONE CHEESE AND WALNUTS

INGREDIENTS
20 round crackers
10 walnuts
3-4 oz of mascarpone

Shell the walnuts and split the kernels in half. With the tip of a knife, spread the mascarpone on cracker, top with half a walnut and arrange side by side on a serving plate. Serve when ready.

31

FIGS
AND MILANO SALAMI

INGREDIENTS
15 fresh figs
4 oz of Milano salami in thick slices

Peel the figs. Split them in two leaving them
joined at the base. In the middle of each fig
place a slice of Milano salami, or if the figs are
small wrap them in salami. Arrange them on a
serving dish. Serve them after they have been
kept in the refrigerator for about an hour.

MOZZARELLA, TOMATO AND BASIL SKEWERS

INGREDIENTS
1 pound of small mozzarella the size of cherry tomatoes
cherry tomatoes
1 handful of basil leaves
wooden skewers

Wash and dry the tomatoes. Drain the mozzarella. Quickly rinse the basil leaves under running water. Put them to dry on a towel. Skewer 1 basil leaf, 1 tomato, and 1 mozzarellina alternating colors until you have all the skewers complete. Place them on a serving dish and serve.

38

For an even more dramatic effect, you can put the skewers inside a round melon or small watermelon

RE

LOVE'S

IS

COLOR

PROSCIUTTO AND MELON ROLLS

INGREDIENTS
$^1/_2$ melon
3 oz of prosciutto in strips

Clean the melon and cut the flesh into cubes. Wrap each cube in a strip of prosciutto and stick it on a toothpick. Arrange on a platter. Serve them after they have been kept in the refrigerator for about 2 hours.

43

FRESHNESS IS THE PROPERTY OF BEING PURE AND NATURAL

SCAMORZA NUGGETS AND PANCETTA

INGREDIENTS
12 smoked scamorza about 1 oz each
2 oz of pancetta steccata cut into strips
2 tablespoons of butter

Wrap each scamorza in a strip of pancetta. Arrange the nuggets on a baking tray. Bake at 350° degrees for a few minutes. Transfer to a serving dish. Serve warm.

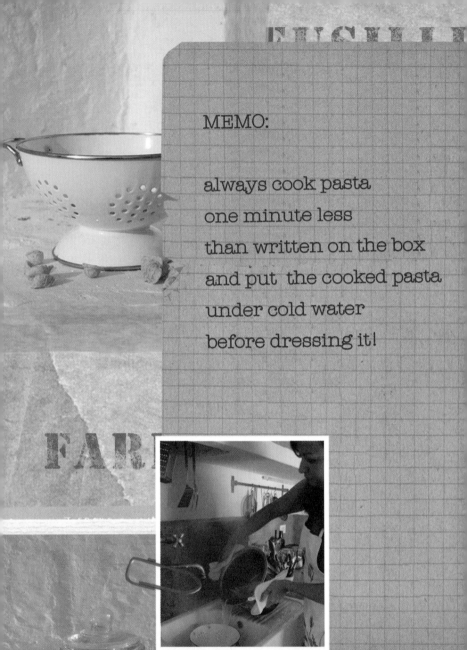

MEMO:

always cook pasta
one minute less
than written on the box
and put the cooked pasta
under cold water
before dressing it!

pasta & rice

FETTUCCINI WITH MEDITERRANEAN HERBS

INGREDIENTS
$3/_4$ oz of fettuccine or noodles
4 tablespoons of marjoram, sage, mint (just a little),
rosemary, thyme, dried and chopped
1 oz of dried porcini mushrooms, chopped
3 oz of smoked pancetta, cut into fairly thick slices
extra virgin olive oil and salt

Mix together the dry Mediterranean herbs, or
prepare them ahead of time. Put them, freshly
picked, on a cardboard tray, and leave them to
dry for 10-15 days. When dry, crumble them
with your hands (remove a few sprigs).
Add them to the chopped dried porcini, and
keep the mixture in a tightly closed glass jar.
In a large frying pan pour 7-8 tablespoons of
oil. Cut the pancetta into small pieces and fry
them in hot oil. Remove them and set aside.
In the same oil put the Mediterranean herbs
and mushrooms. Leave them on the flame for
one minute for flavor, and then turn off the
heat.
Boil the noodles to al dente. Drain them. Add
them to the pan with the oil and herbs. Add the
bacon. Stir quickly, and serve.

52

53

STEP 1

You can use
fresh or dried
aromatic herbs

54

STEP 2

STEP 3

55

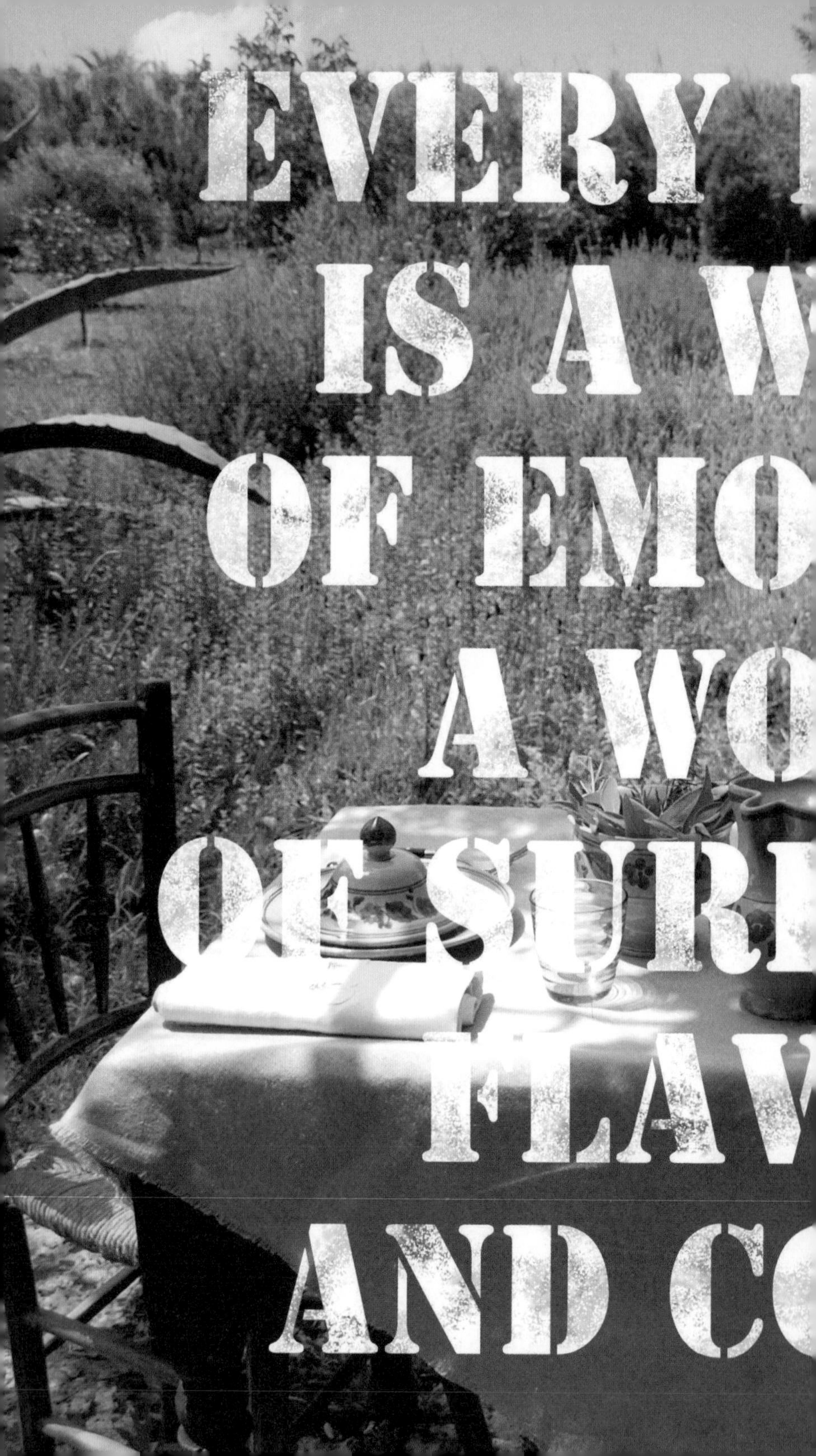

EVERY

IS A W

OF EMO

A WO

OF SUR

FLAV

AND CO

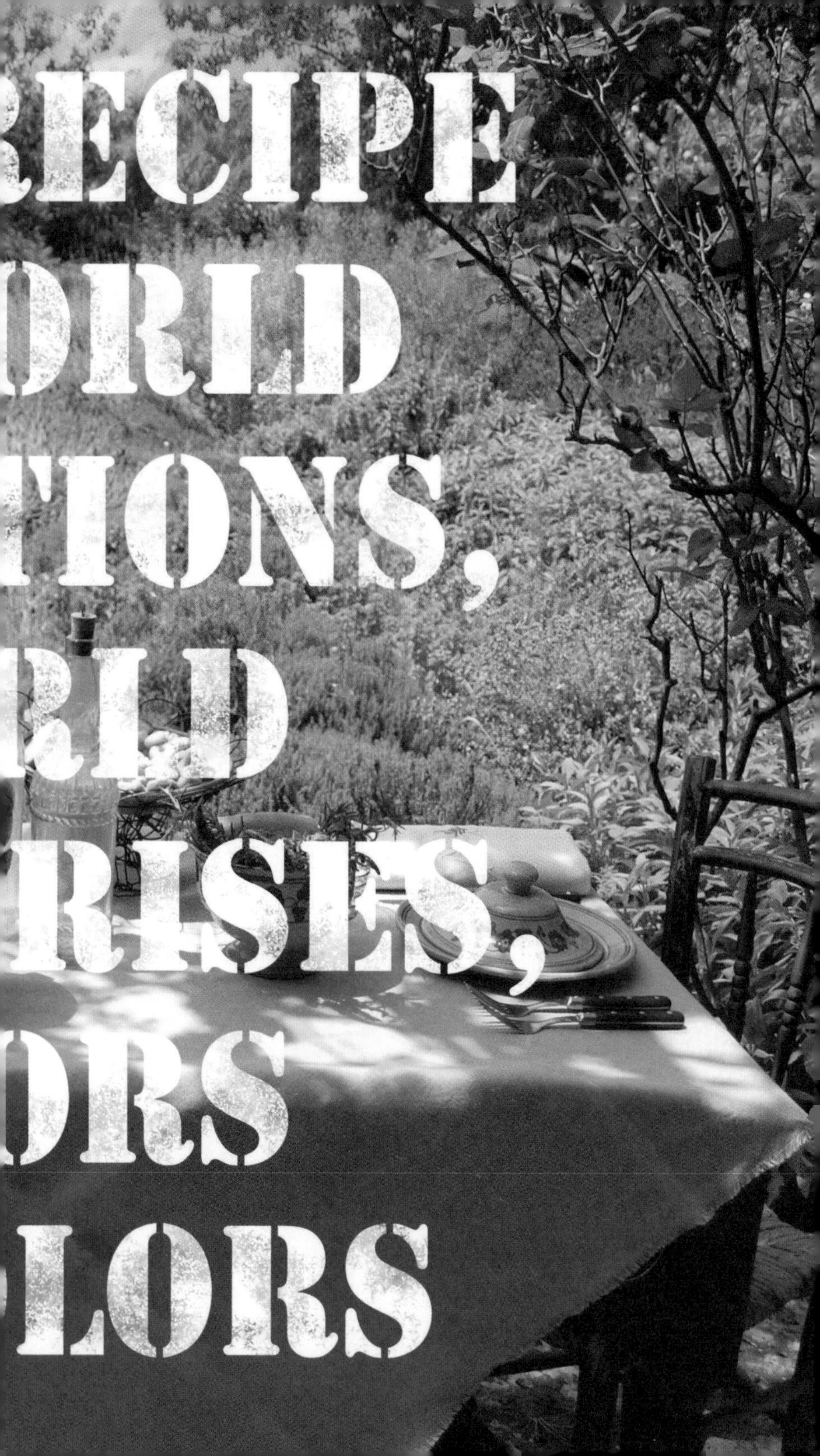

ECIPE
ORLD
TIONS,
RID
RISES,
ORS
LORS

FUSILLI "ALLA CAPRESE"

INGREDIENTS
$^3/_4$ pound fusilli
$^3/_4$ pound mozzarella
1 pound cherry tomatoes
15-20 fresh basil leaves
extra virgin olive oil and salt to taste

Cut the tomatoes into wedges and dice the
mozzarella. Put them in a bowl and add oil and
chopped basil. Boil the pasta al dente in salted
water, drain and pour into the pan with the
sauce. Stir and garnish with a sprig of fresh
basil.

58

To release the scent
and flavor of the basil,
break it up with your hands

59

You can use cherry tomatoes in the winter
and plum-tomatoes in the summer

62

HUNGER IS

SAUCE IN T

HOMEMADE ORECCHIETTE

INGREDIENTS
1 pound of semolina
water

Put the flour on a pastry board. Add as much water as it will take to get a fairly thick dough. Knead the dough energetically and for a long time. Make rolls of dough $\frac{1}{2}$ inch in diameter, and cut into 1 inch segments. Hollow out each stub of pasta with the smooth and rounded tip of a knife. Quickly turn it over so that the outer part is rough. Lay the orecchiette on a towel to dry.

Add flour to your hands if you feel them sticky

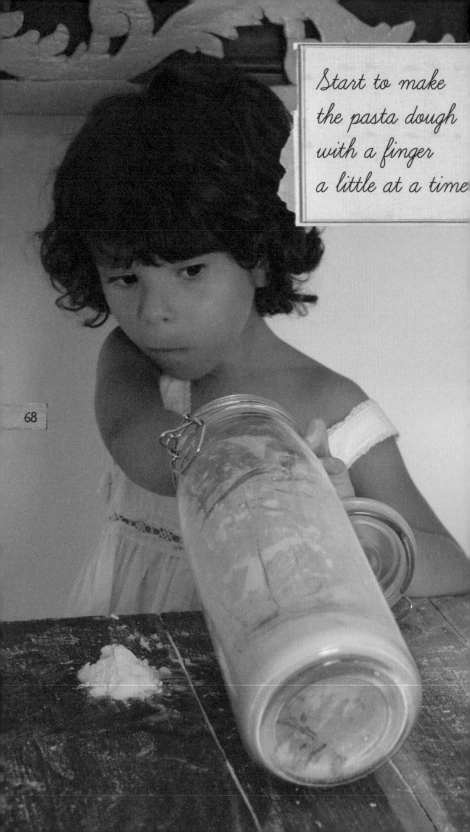

Start to make
the pasta dough
with a finger
a little at a time

69

ORECCHIETTE "ALLA CRUDAIOLA"

INGREDIENTS
1 pound of fleshy, ripe tomatoes
5 oz of arugula or 20-25 basil leaves
extra virgin olive oil and salt to taste
10 oz of grated or flaked ricotta cheese or cubed
mozzarella

Wash the tomatoes and cut them into cubes. In
a large frying pan pour 7-8 tablespoons of olive
oil. When smoking add the tomatoes, salt, and
cook for 5 minutes stirring occasionally. With
the flame off add the arugula or basil. Cook the
orecchiette pasta. Drain it. Add them to the
pan with the tomatoes. Let it cook for two
minutes. Serve with a sprinkling of ricotta
cheese or cubes of mozzarella.

ORECCHIETTE WITH BROCCOLI OR BROCCOLI RABE

INGREDIENTS
4 pounds broccoli or broccoli rabe
2 cloves of garlic
2 teaspoons of anchovy paste
$\frac{1}{2}$ teaspoon of crushed red pepper, to taste
extra virgin olive oil and salt to taste

Cut the softest tops of broccoli rabe or broccoli. Wash and drain them. Boil them in salted water until they are al dente. Drain them. In a large frying pan pour 7-8 tablespoons of olive oil. Add the garlic and anchovy paste. When the garlic is golden, add the vegetables. Cook them, and let season for 3-4 minutes. Cook the orecchiette pasta. Drain it and add to the pan. Sprinkle with pepper. Stir and serve.

A TRADITIC
BELIEF OR
PASSED DO
A GROUP O
WITH SYMI
MEANING O
SIGNIFICAN
ORIGINS IN

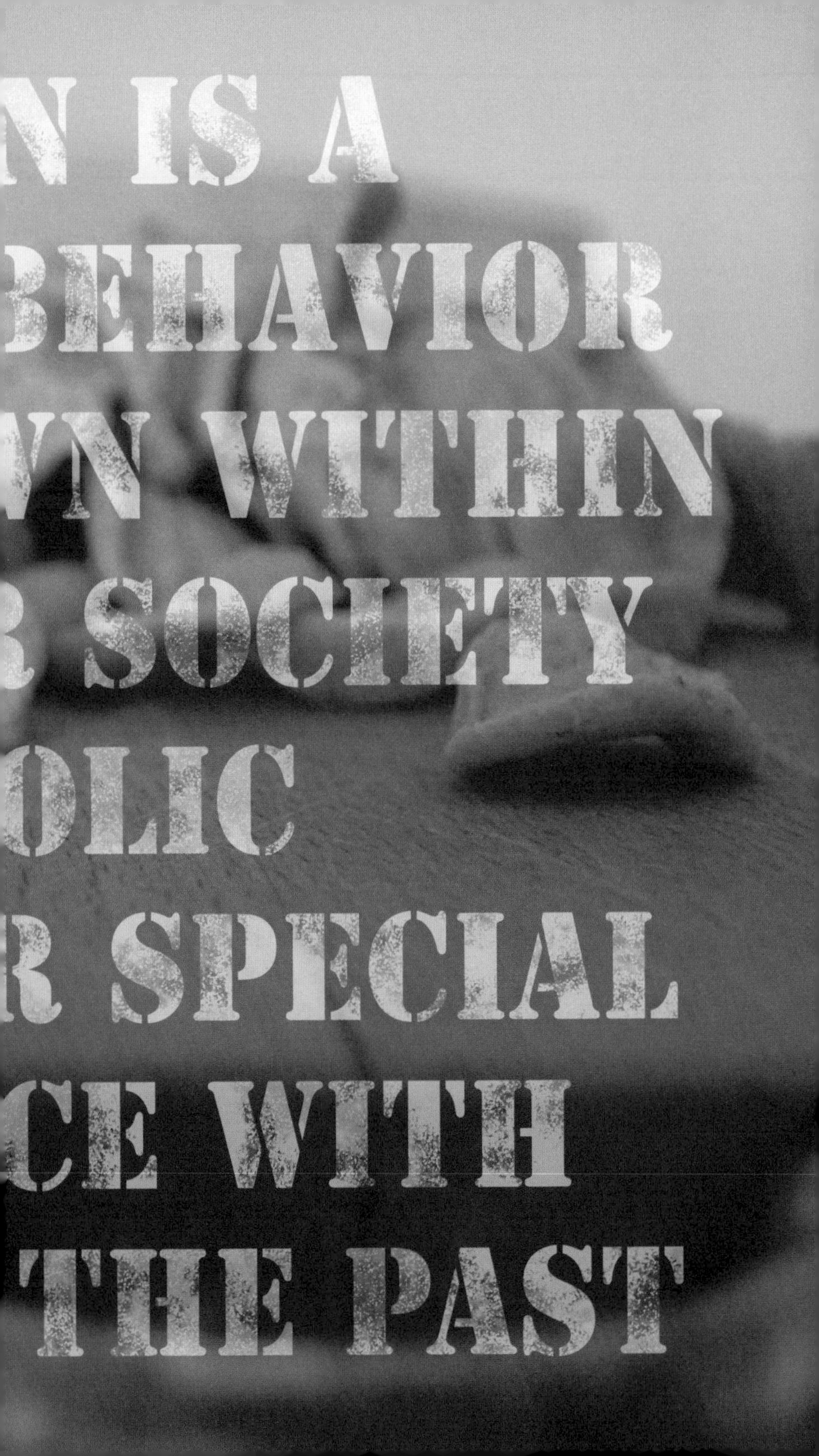

N IS A
BEHAVIOR
WN WITHIN
R SOCIETY
OLIC
R SPECIAL
CE WITH
THE PAST

LINGUINE
WITH
ROASTED TOMATOES

INGREDIENTS
$^3/_4$ pound of spaghetti
2 pounds of ripe cherry tomatoes
1 cup of bread crumbs
1 clove of garlic
1 bunch of parsley
a lot of basil
2 tablespoons of oregano
extra virgin olive oil and salt to taste
Coarsely grated ricotta or cottage cheese (to taste)

74 Take a shallow roasting pan (baking sheet). Using the flat edge of a large knife, crush a clove of garlic to remove the skin and place on the bottom of the pan. Pour a little oil in the pan. Cut the tomatoes in half and lay them in the pan side by side, very compact, with the cut side up. Sprinkle them with salt.
In a bowl, mix the bread crumbs with the oregano, basil and finely chopped parsley. Mix these ingredients well with your hands. Sprinkle the tomatoes with the mixture. Drizzle them with olive oil, and place them in a preheated oven at 350° for 45 minutes. Remove them from the oven when they are au gratin. Cook the pasta al dente, drain and toss with the tomatoes. Serve immediately with plenty of cheese.

76

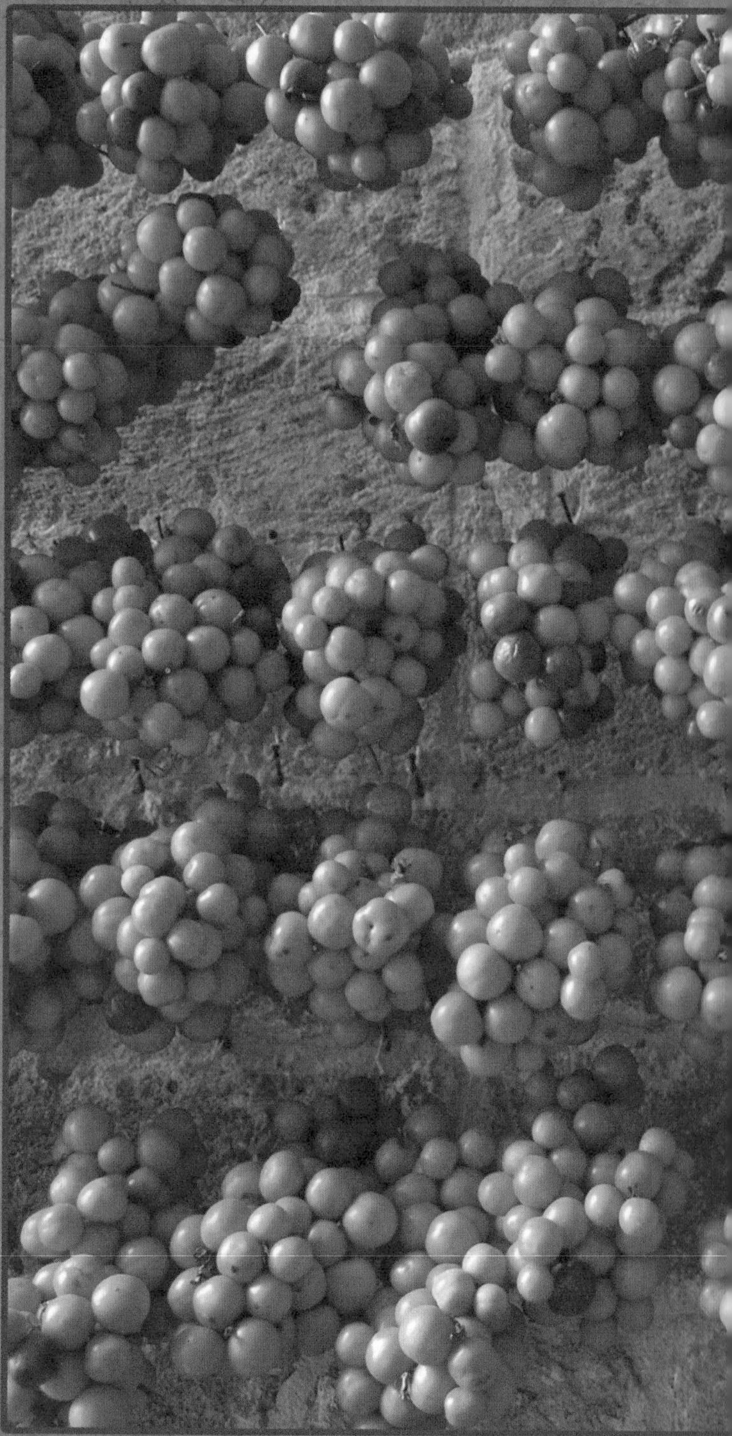

PENNE
WITH PESTO
AND CHERRY TOMATOES

INGREDIENTS
$3/4$ pound of penne rigate
15-20 fleshy, ripe tomatoes
extra virgin olive oil and salt and to taste
5 tablespoons of pesto

Pour the pesto into a bowl. Add the diced
tomatoes. Cook the penne rigate until al dente
in salted water. Drain it, and add them to the
sauce. Stir and serve.

STEP 1

Add 2-3 tablespoons of pine nuts and a few leaves of fresh basil in the pasta sauce

STEP 3

85

FINAL TOUCH

PENNE WITH RICOTTA, ZUCCHINI AND MINT

INGREDIENTS
$^3/_4$ pound of pasta (penne or reginette or tripoline)
$^3/_4$ pound of zucchini
1 pound of ricotta cheese
salt to taste
oil for frying
1 handful of fresh mint leaves

Cut the zucchini into slices. Season with salt.
Fry in hot oil. Drain and place them on paper
towels. Set them aside.
Put the ricotta in a bowl. Add 3–4 tablespoons
of hot water. Temper with the tines of a fork.
Cook the pasta in plenty of boiling salted water.
Drain and put it in a bowl. Add the ricotta
cheese, zucchini and mint. Stir. Garnish with
mint leaves and serve.

You can use
another creamy cheese
instead of ricotta cheese

89

RIGATONI WITH GRILLED VEGETABLES

INGREDIENTS
$^3/_4$ pound of rigatoni
2 eggplants
1 yellow pepper
7-8 zucchini
1 clove of garlic
15-20 basil leaves
extra virgin olive oil and salt to taste

Prick the zucchini skin with a fork, slice
lengthwise and grill on a cast iron plate.
Roast the whole eggplant and the pepper
separately on red-hot coals or on a griddle.
Seal in plastic bags to let them cool. Remove
skins and divide into strips, discarding pepper
seeds. Boil the pasta to al dente in salted water,
drain and toss in bowl with a clove of crushed
garlic, zucchini, pepper and chopped basil.
Season with plenty of olive oil, serve either hot
or at room temperature.

93

94

STEP 1

STEP 2

95

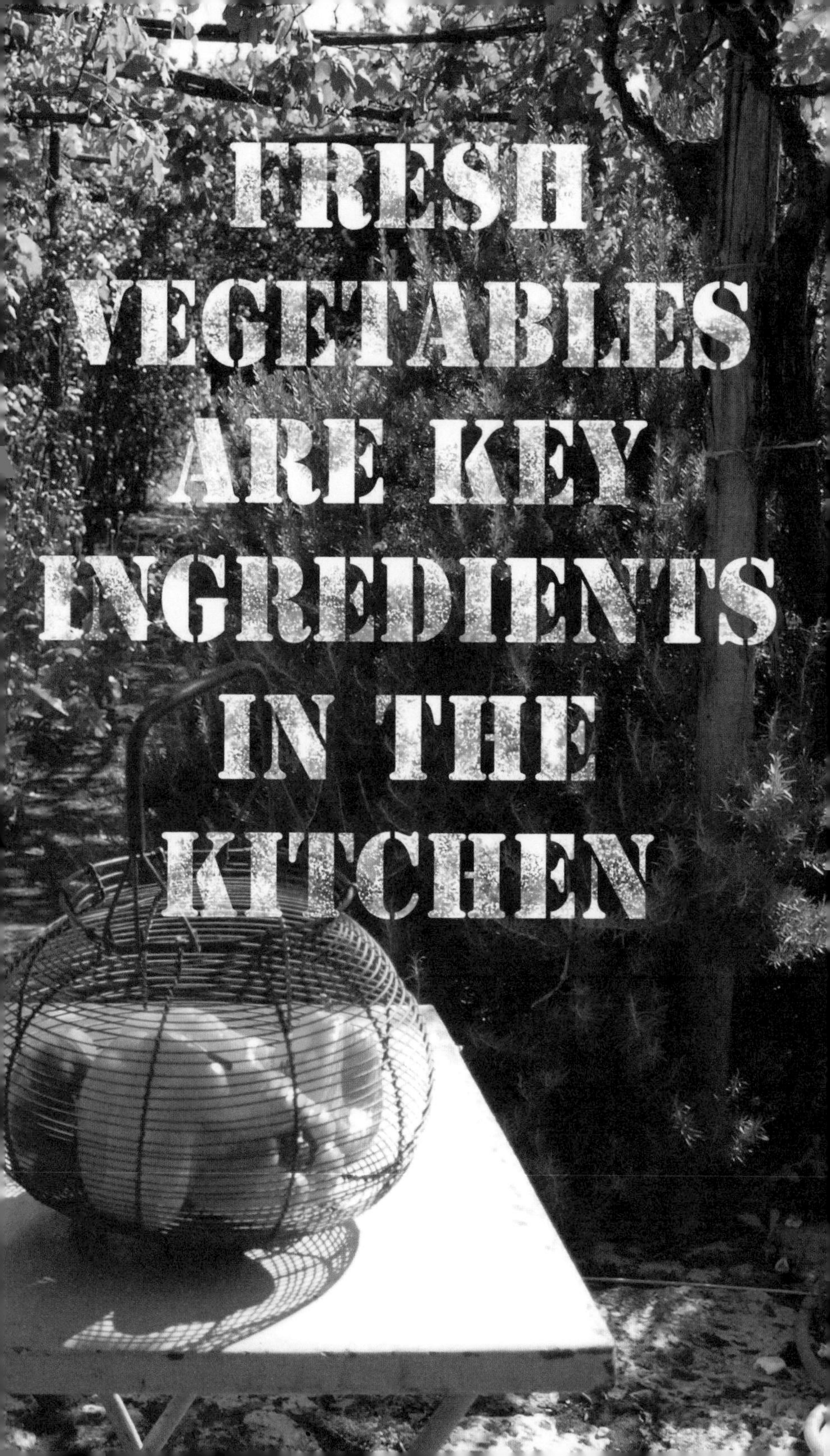
FRESH VEGETABLES ARE KEY INGREDIENTS IN THE KITCHEN

RISOTTO "ALLA MILANESE"

INGREDIENTS
1 $\frac{1}{2}$ cups of Carnaroli rice
8 tablespoons of butter
4 tablespoons of grated Parmesan cheese
1 white onion
$\frac{1}{2}$ cup of dry white wine
2 cups of beef broth
1 sachet of saffron
extra virgin olive oil and salt to taste

Peel and finely chop the onion cooking over low heat in a saucepan with 3 oz of butter and 4-5 tablespoons of oil. Add the rice, and let it sautee. Add the wine, and let it evaporate. Pour the broth one ladle at a time and only when the previous one has been completely absorbed. Stir often.
When the rice is almost cooked, add the saffron which should be dissolved in a little broth first. Season with salt, stir, turn, incorporating half of the Parmesan cheese. Cover and let it stand for 2-3 minutes. Transfer to a risottiera. (or a large plate). Add the remaining Parmesan cheese and butter. Stir and serve.

99

RISOTTO WITH MUSHROOMS

INGREDIENTS
1 ¹/₂ cups of rice
1 pound of frozen (or fresh) mushrooms
2 oz of dried porcini mushrooms
4 cups of mushroom or vegetable broth
1 clove of garlic
1 medium onion, white
4 tablespoons of butter
1 glass of dry white wine
4 tablespoons chopped parsley
2 tablespoons of parmesan cheese
extra virgin olive oil and salt to taste

Soak the dried mushrooms in warm water for 10-15 minutes. Squeeze and chop them, set the soaking water aside. In a frying pan, pour 4-5 tablespoons of olive oil, sauté a clove of fresh garlic, add all the mushrooms (frozen or fresh and reconstituted dried ones). Cook for 10-12 minutes, set aside. In a saucepan, pour 2-3 tablespoons of olive oil, half the butter, chopped onion, and sauté until brown. Add rice, stirring constantly, until toasted. Pour in wine and let evaporate. Continue cooking, adding mushroom water and then broth, one ladle at a time and only when previous one has been completely absorbed, stirring continuously. Add mushrooms when rice is almost cooked (approximately 25-30 minutes or between al dente and tender). Cook for 5 more minutes, then turn off heat. Stir in remaining butter, let sit in covered pan for 5 minutes. Sprinkle with chopped parsley and transfer to a risottiera (or large plate) and serve. Offer cheese at the table for those who like it.

WHITE IS LIGHT. A STRONG AND DAZZLING LIGHT TO BE ALMOST TANGIBLE, LIVING MATTER

SPAGHETTI "ALLA CARBONARA"

INGREDIENTS
$3/4$ pound of spaghetti
5 oz of smoked pancetta or guanciale, diced
the yolks of four fresh eggs
2 oz of parmesan or pecorino cheese, grated
extra virgin olive oil, salt and pepper to taste

In a frying pan with a little oil cook the diced
pancetta or guanciale for about 5 minutes,
until it is lightly browned.
Whisk the egg yolks and the cheese together in
a bowl with a fork adding a sprinkling of
freshly ground black pepper.
Cook the spaghetti al-dente in boiling salted
water. Drain it, and pour into the bowl with the
beaten eggs. Add the bacon. Stir quickly so that
the eggs do not set. Serve immediately.

104

You can add two
tablespoons of milk or
cream if you prefer the
sauce not too dry

106

SPAGHETTI WITH CLAMS

$3/4$ pound of spaghetti
2 pounds of clams
2 cloves of garlic
10-12 fresh tomatoes
crushed red pepper
chopped parsley
extra virgin olive oil and salt to taste

Leave the clams to soak and change the water several times. Then put them in a pot over medium heat until they open. Remove the clam from the shell for half, leaving the other half still in the shell. Filter the cooking water. In a shallow pan put 7-8 tablespoons of olive oil and two cloves of garlic. Fry the garlic until golden and mix in the clams. Add the tomatoes, a pinch of crushed red pepper, the filtered cooking water and cook for five minutes over high heat. Cook the spaghetti al dente. Drain it and transfer to a serving dish. Pour over the clams with their sauce. Sprinkle with plenty of finely chopped parsley and serve.

SPAGHETTI WITH MEATBALLS

$^3/_4$ pound of pasta (spaghetti or another kind of pasta)
2 oz of grated cheese, to taste

For the sauce:
3 cups of tomato sauce
$^1/_2$ onion
5-6 basil leaves
Extra virgin olive oil and salt to taste

For the meatballs:
1 pound of veal, coarsely ground
1 teaspoon salt
1 egg
2 tablespoons of grated Parmesan cheese
6 slices of bread
1 sprig of parsley finely chopped
1 pinch of pepper

For the meatballs:
Remove the crust from the bread and wet with water. Squeeze it, and combine it in a bowl with the other ingredients. Mix well by hand until the dough is quite soft and form into balls the size of a walnut. Put aside in a dish.

For the sauce:
In a pan pour 5-6 tablespoons of oil. Add the finely sliced onion. When sizzling add the tomato puree, salt and cook for about 15 minutes flavoring with basil. Gently place the balls in the sauce and let it cook for 15 -20 mins. Cook the pasta al dente. Season it with the sauce, meatballs and a sprinkling of Parmesan cheese or hard ricotta, as desired. The meatballs can also be deep fried in extra virgin olive oil and served as a main dish or as an appetizer.

STEP 1

The meatballs,
before combining
them with
the tomato sauce,
can be fried in
hot oil

TAGLIATELLE "ALLA BOLOGNESE"

INGREDIENTS
$^3/_4$ pound of pasta (tagliatelle or fettuccine)
1 pound of ground meat (half beef and half pork)
1 carrot
1 stalk of celery
$^1/_2$ onion
2 bay leaves
$^1/_2$ glass of red wine
3 cups of tomato sauce
extra virgin olive oil, salt and pepper to taste
2 oz of thin slices of mortadella, to taste
Parmesan cheese, to taste

118

In a saucepan pour $^1/_2$ cup of oil. Add the cleaned, washed, dried and finely chopped vegetables. Brown them over medium heat. Add the meat and crumble it with a fork. Fry for 3-4 minutes. Add the wine and let it evaporate. Add the tomato sauce, bay leaves and cook the "Bolognese" for about 40 minutes over a low heat. Remove from heat. Stir in the strips of mortadella. Sprinkle with pepper. Stir and let it sit for five minutes.

Cook the noodles al dente. Drain and dress with the sauce. Serve to taste, with Parmesan cheese grated at the table.

To have white Bolognese, just do not add the tomato sauce

TUNA, PEPPER AND EGGPLANT SPAGHETTI

INGREDIENTS
$^3/_4$ pound spaghetti
1 clove of garlic
1 medium-sized eggplant
3 green peppers (horn)
3 tablespoons of pitted green olives
3 tablespoons of pitted black olives
$^1/_2$ pound tuna in oil
1 pound peeled tomatoes in pieces
crushed hot chili pepper (to taste)
extra virgin olive oil and salt to taste

Clean, wash and cut the peppers into strips
and dice the eggplant. In a pan, put 5-6 tablespoons of olive oil, 1 clove of garlic, and when it
is golden, add the vegetables and fry them.
Add the tomatoes and let them cook for about
10 minutes. Remove from heat, add the tuna,
olives and crushed hot chili pepper (to taste).
Cook the spaghetti al dente in salted water.
Drain and transfer to a bowl with the sauce.

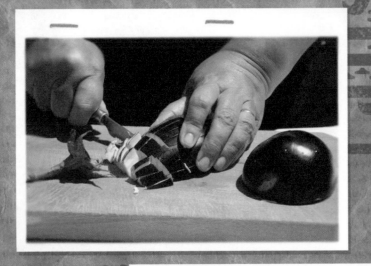

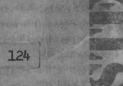

THE BEST
IN TH

IS THE CAI

OF A GOO

MEDICINE
E END

MING FOOD
D FRIEND

MEMO:

Beans are cooked best
in "pignate" – special
fire-resistant
terracotta pots

legumes &
vegetables

A SIMPLE DISH IS THE RIGHT DIRECTION, IF YOU COOK IT TO PERFECTION

BITTERSWEET ENDIVES

INGREDIENTS
4 heads of Belgian endives
1 lemon or 4-5 tablespoons of apple cider vinegar
3 tablespoons of raisins
3 tablespoons of pine nuts
2 tablespoons of large Parmesan cheese flakes, to taste
extra virgin olive oil and salt to taste

Put the raisins in warm water for 20 minutes
to soften them.
Lightly toast the pine nuts.
In a bowl place the cut, washed, drained,
squeezed endives. Add the raisins and pine
nuts. Season with lemon juice or apple cider
vinegar, salt and oil. Sprinkle with Parmesan
cheese and serve.

134

Do not cut the endive long before serving it, because otherwise the leaves blacken

EGGPLANT PARMIGIANA

INGREDIENTS
4-5 medium-sized eggplants
4 oz of grated Parmesan cheese
4 cups of fresh tomato sauce with basil and meatballs
10 oz of caciocavallo cheese
extra virgin olive oil and salt to taste

For the meatballs:
10 oz of ground beef meat
$1/_2$ cup of bread crumbs
1 oz of grated pecorino cheese
1 tablespoon of grated Parmesan cheese
chopped parsley
1 egg
1 clove of garlic
salt and pepper to taste
4 cups of extra virgin olive oil

Cut the eggplant into slices, and place in a container in layers with salt. Leave for two hours so that it will lose its water and bitter taste. Fry them.
Make the meatballs the size of a hazelnut after having mixed the ingredients. Fry them and leave for 10 minutes in boiling tomato sauce.
In a pan pour 2 ladles of tomato sauce. Place a layer of eggplant, sliced cheese, meatballs in tomato sauce, and Parmesan cheese. Finish with eggplant, tomato sauce, and sprinkle with grated cheese. Cook in the oven at 350° for about half an hour.

FAVA BEANS
AND CHICORY

INGREDIENTS
1 pound of fava beans
1 clove of garlic
2-3 bay leaves
$\frac{1}{2}$ onion
3-4 tomatoes
1 sprig of parsley
1 potato
2 pounds of wild chicory (already cleaned)
extra virgin olive oil and salt to taste

Removing the rind, soak the fava beans the
night before. Cook them in salted water over
low heat in an uncovered clay pot with a clove
of garlic, 2-3 bay leaves, onion, 3-4 tomatoes, a
sprig of parsley, and a peeled whole potato.
Once cooked, pass them through a food mill.
Wash the chicory several times, and boil it in
salted water. Spread the pureed fava beans at
the center of a platter, add the chicory on top
and serve immediately with plenty of olive oil.

GREEN BEANS
AND SAUTEED POTATOES

INGREDIENTS
1 $^1/_4$ pounds of beans
1 $^1/_2$ pounds of potatoes
extra virgin olive oil and salt to taste

Wash the potatoes. Boil them. When they have
cooled a little, peel and cut into cubes.
Clean the beans trimming them and eliminate
the filaments. Wash and boil them in salted
water.
In a large frying pan pour half a cup of oil. Over
medium heat, sauté the potatoes, fry and
transfer them to the center of a serving dish.
Sauté the beans and place them all around the
potatoes. Serve.

143

STEP 2

STEP 1

Run the beans under cold water to stop the cooking and keep them crisp when cooked

GRILLED EGGPLANT WITH MINT

INGREDIENTS
3-4 medium-sized eggplants
1-2 cloves of garlic
1 handful of mint
7-8 tablespoons white wine or apple cider vinegar
Extra virgin olive oil and salt to taste

Wash the eggplant. Pat dry and cut into pieces
2-3 inches in length and place in a large bowl.
Season with salt, vinegar, oil, and rub them
between your hands so that you give them a
good seasoning.
Line a baking sheet with parchment paper.
Place the eggplants and cook in a preheated
oven at 350° on the top shelf for about half an
hour until the eggplants are soft and golden.
Transfer them to a serving dish. Flavor them
with mint and garlic. Let them sit for at least
an hour and serve.

147

POTATOES
AND ARTICHOKES

INGREDIENTS
10 artichokes
1 lemon
6 large potatoes
5 tablespoons of grated cheese
$2/_3$ cup of bread crumbs
abundant parsley
1 clove of garlic
extra virgin olive oil, salt and pepper to taste

Clean the artichokes by removing the hard outer leaves, trimming the top and pointed tips of remaining leaves. Remove the hair above the heart if necessary. Slice lengthwise and soak in water acidified with lemon juice.
Clean and peel the potatoes. Cut into thin horizontal slices. Soak them in salted water. Mix the bread, cheese, chopped parsley, and freshly ground black pepper in a bowl. Grease the bottom of a baking dish with the garlic and a little olive oil. Place a layer of potatoes, then bread crumbs mixed with cheese, parsley and pepper. Add a little olive oil, and then place a layer of artichokes. Add another layer of the mixture of bread crumbs and cheese. Finish with a layer of potatoes sprinkle with crumbs and grated cheese. Season with oil. Add water up to the last layer of potatoes. Bake at 180° for about an hour until the artichokes and potatoes are cooked. The cooking water dries on the surface and will have formed a golden brown and crispy crust.

149

SALAD OF ARUGULA, FIGS AND PRIMO SALE

INGREDIENTS
1 pound of rocket (arugula)
1 pound of fresh figs
5 oz of primo sale or another fresh cheese cut into small pieces
extra virgin olive oil and salt to taste

Break up the tender leaves of rocket by hand.
Wash again, and drain them.
Put them in a bowl. Add the figs peeled and cut in half if small, or wedges, if larger.
Add the pieces of the primo sale. Season with salt and oil. Stir. Leave to flavor for fifteen minutes and serve.

STEWED LENTILS

INGREDIENTS
10 oz of lentils
$^1/_2$ onion
1 stalk of celery
1 carrot
2 bay leaves
1 stock [bouillon] cube
extra virgin olive oil to taste

Soak the lentils in water for 7-8 hours. Add
enough water to cover the lentils, season with
a bouillon cube and bring to a boil. In another
pan add 7-8 tablespoons of oil. Stir in the
chopped onion, celery, and carrot. When the oil
sizzles and vegetables are golden, add the
lentils and 2 bay leaves. Continue cooking for
15 -20 minutes. Serve hot.

157

159

Add half a
teaspoon of baking
soda in the water
with the lentils
to shorten
cooking time

SWEET AND SOUR BAKED ONIONS

INGREDIENTS
3 pounds of small white onions, roughly the same size
1 cup of white wine vinegar
sugar to taste
extra virgin olive oil and salt to taste

Cut the onions horizontally in half, and blanch them in boiling salted water. Drain them. Remove the outer skins and lay them, side by side, in a pan lined with parchment paper. On each half onion (cut side facing up) put a half teaspoon of sugar, a dash of vinegar, and a little olive oil. Bake in a preheated oven at 200° until golden. Transfer to a serving dish. Serve at room temperature.

Use red onions if
you prefer
a sweeter taste

164

VEGETABLES
AU GRATIN

INGREDIENTS
7-8 zucchini
1 yellow pepper
7-8 medium sized potatoes
$1/_4$ cup of bread crumbs
extra virgin olive oil and salt to taste

Peel the potatoes. Chop the zucchini. Cut the
pepper into strips. Then cut all the vegetables
into pieces the same size, and keep them in salt
water for 10 minutes.
Line a shallow roasting pan with parchment
paper. Lay just one layer of the drained
vegetables. Sprinkle with plenty of bread
crumbs and
season with a little oil. Place in an oven
preheated to 400° and bake for about 45
minutes until the vegetables are cooked,
browned and crispy.

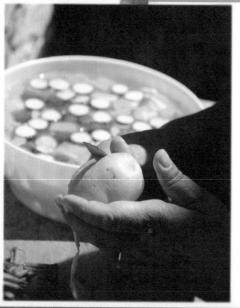

SUNWASHED = WARMED BY THE DIRECT RAYS OF THE SUN

MEMO:

Wash dishes dirty
from egg
with cold water
and vinegar
to remove the smell

SALT

OIL

FLOUR

eggs
& omelettes

ARTICHOKE
(OR ASPARAGUS)
FRITTATA

INGREDIENTS
10 artichoke hearts sliced thin (or 20 asparagus)
4 eggs
6-7 tablespoons of grated Parmesan cheese
$1/_2$ cup of bread crumbs
4 tablespoons chopped parsley
extra virgin olive oil, salt and pepper to taste

Pour 6 tablespoons of olive oil into a pan. When
hot, add the artichokes (or asparagus) and
cook over high heat. Let them cool. Place them
in a bowl, and add the eggs, cheese, bread,
parsley, salt and pepper and mix all the
ingredients with a fork.
In a large pan, pour 5-6 tablespoons of olive oil.
When hot, pour in the mixture with artichokes
(or asparagus). Lower the heat, and cook the
omelette until golden on one side. With the
help of a lid flip it over and finish cooking.
Slide it on a plate with a paper towel to dry the
excess oil. Transfer it to a serving dish and
serve either warm or at room temperature.

EGGS IN PURGATORY

INGREDIENTS
2 leeks
6 eggs
pepper, to taste
extra virgin olive oil and salt to taste

Peel the leeks and cut them into chunks lengthwise. In a saucepan heat 4-5 tablespoons of oil. Add the leeks and cook over medium heat.
In a bowl beat the eggs with a pinch of salt and pepper. Pour the eggs over the leeks and thicken. Serve hot.

179

EGGS WITH TOMATOES

INGREDIENTS
4 eggs
1 leek
8-10 ripe tomatoes
8-10 basil leaves
extra virgin olive oil and salt to taste

Wash the tomatoes. Remove seeds and chop. In a pan pour 5-6 tablespoons of oil. Add the leek cut into thin slices, and sautee over a low flame. Add the tomatoes, basil and cook gently for 10-15 minutes. Break the eggs onto the tomato-leek mixture, well-spaced from one another. Cover with a lid and cook a few seconds until the egg whites but not the yolks have thickened. Serve very hot eggs accompanied with slices of homemade bread.

181

FRIED EGGPLANT FRITTERS

INGREDIENTS
3 medium-sized eggplants
1 clove of garlic
3 eggs
$1/_3$ cup of bread crumbs
2 tablespoons of grated cheese (Parmesan and pecorino)
1 bunch of parsley
$2/_3$ tablespoon pickled capers (to taste)
salt and pepper to taste
fine bread crumbs
extra virgin olive oil for frying

Cut the unpeeled eggplant into large pieces and boil in salted water. Drain well, and squeeze with your hands. Put them in a bowl and add the eggs, bread crumbs, grated cheese, finely chopped parsley, crushed garlic, capers and fresh ground pepper. Mix all the ingredients well and make pancakes in the desired form (balls, fritters or croquettes). Cover in fine bread crumbs and fry in hot oil. Serve the fritters hot or at room temperature.

STEP 3

STEP 5

FRIED VEGETABLES

INGREDIENTS
7-8 zucchini
2 medium eggplants
12 fresh sage leaves

For the batter:
6 tablespoons of sifted flour
$1/2$ cup of carbonated water
1 tablespoon of olive oil
2 egg whites, beaten stiff
$1/2$ teaspoon of salt
1 quart of extra virgin olive oil for frying

188

Clean, wash, cut zucchini and eggplant into sticks. Sprinkle with a little salt, and let them sit for an hour on a cutting board to remove the water. Wash and dry the sage leaves.

For the batter:
Put the flour in a bowl, add oil and carbonated water. Beat with a fork until batter is smooth and let it rest for an hour. Then, in a separate bowl, beat egg whites until stiff and gently fold into the flour mixture.
In a deep pan pour the oil. When hot, fry a few at a time starting first with the zucchini, then the sage, then the eggplant, after first being dipped in the batter.
When golden brown, remove them from the oil with a wooden spoon a few at a time.
Let them dry on paper towels. Serve hot.

189

FRITTATA
WITH MINT

INGREDIENTS
4 eggs
2 tablespoons of grated pecorino cheese
2 tablespoons of grated Parmesan cheese
5 tablespoons of bread crumbs
2 tablespoons of milk
a bunch of parsley
1 clove of garlic
20-25 mint leaves
extra virgin olive oil, salt and pepper to taste

In a bowl beat the eggs with pecorino,
Parmesan, bread crumbs, milk, chopped
parsley, a pinch of finely chopped garlic,
chopped mint, salt and pepper.
Put a little oil in a large pan, and, when hot,
pour in the mixture.
Lower the heat and cook on one side. Then
turn over the omelette to the other side with
the help of a lid to finish cooking.
Set it on a paper towel to remove any excess
oil. Serve immediately.

191

THERE IS
BETWEEN I
COLO
NUTRITIO
THERE IS
CULT
PREFEREN
COLOR OVE

NO LINK

G'S SHELL

AND

AL VALUE,

OFTEN A

URAL

E FOR ONE

ANOTHER

PASTA FRITTATA

INGREDIENTS
10 oz of left over pasta topped with tomato sauce
3 eggs
4 tablespoons grated Parmesan cheese
2 tablespoons of grated pecorino cheese
8 tablespoons of bread crumbs
3 tablespoons chopped parsley
extra virgin olive oil, salt and pepper to taste

Coarsely chop the left over pasta and place in a bowl. Add eggs, bread crumbs, grated cheese, parsley and a generous sprinkling of freshly ground black pepper. Mix the ingredients together and season with salt.
In a frying pan pour 6-7 tablespoons of olive oil. When hot, pour the mixture to coagulate. Lower the heat and cook the omelet on one side, with the help of a lid turn the omelet. Cook the other side. When it is golden and crisp slide it onto a paper towel to remove excess grease. Transfer it to a serving dish. Serve hot or at room temperature.

195

POTATO CROQUETTES

INGREDIENTS
2 pounds of potatoes
2 tablespoons of grated Parmesan cheese
$1/4$ cup of bread crumbs
3 eggs
chopped parsley or mint
salt and pepper to taste
$1/2$ pound of fine bread crumbs
extra virgin olive oil for frying

Boil the potatoes and mash them.
Mix the mashed potatoes with Parmesan and
bread crumbs, chopped parsley (or mint), eggs,
salt and pepper. Form a stick, with a diameter
of $1/2$ inch and 3 inches long, to a rounded
point at each end. Dust with very finely grated
bread crumbs and fry them in hot oil. Serve
the croquettes hot.

197

198

199

A LUCKY
PERSON IS
SOMEONE
WHO PLANTS
PEBBLES
AND
HARVESTS
POTATOES

CHIC

COI

SAUS

LAMI

BBIT

MEMO:

The various types
and cuts of meat
require particular
times and methods
of cooking

meat

FLAVOR IS BASED MAINLY ON THE SENSE OF TASTE AND SMELL

BAKED LAMB

INGREDIENTS
3 pounds of lamb (preferably thigh)
2 -3 bay leaves
4-5 leaves of sage
2 sprigs of rosemary
2 cloves of garlic, whole
2 pounds of potatoes
$\frac{1}{4}$ cup of bread crumbs
2 tablespoons of parsley, chopped
extra virgin olive oil and salt to taste

Cut the lamb into pieces and put them to soak in water, salt, garlic, olive oil, bay leaves, rosemary, and sage for at least 3-4 hours. Then place them in a baking dish. Sprinkle with 2 ladles of the marinade. Distribute the potatoes, peeled and cut into slices. Sprinkle with bread crumbs and chopped parsley. Drizzle with a little olive oil. Place in preheated oven at 400° and bake for about an hour until lamb and potatoes are thoroughly cooked and browned.

STEP 2

STEP 3

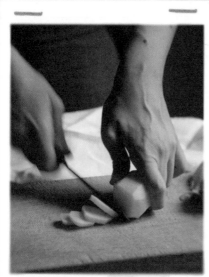

211

BREADED SCHIACCIATINE

INGREDIENTS
For the dough:
$^1/_2$ pound ground veal
$^1/_2$ pound ground pork
1 clove of garlic
6-7 tablespoons grated Parmesan cheese
1 egg
1 tablespoon chopped parsley
$^2/_3$ cup of bread crumbs
2 tablespoons milk
salt and pepper to taste

For the breading:
6-7 table spoons extra virgin olive oil
$^1/_2$ cup of fine bread crumbs

In a bowl, on the bottom of which the garlic has
been rubbed, put all of the ingredients and
knead with your hands until it is well blended.
Make the patties. Put the oil in a dish and the
bread crumbs in another. Put the schiacciatine
first in the oil and then in the bread crumbs.
Mash them well between your hands, so that
they have a compact form and the bread
crumbs adhere well to the dough. Grill them
on a hot plate until fully cooked.

214

STEP 5

CHICKEN WITH BEER

INGREDIENTS
4 chicken thighs
6 tablespoons of flour
1 clove of garlic
1 can of sweet beer
1 tablespoon of pepper berries
1 sprig of rosemary
2-3 bay leaves
3-4 leaves of sage
extra virgin olive oil and salt to taste

Strip the chicken legs, and split them into
upper thighs and ends. Add salt and flour.
In a large pot pour $1/2$ cup of olive oil. Add a
clove of garlic. When the garlic is browned
place the chicken pieces in a single layer.
Cook and brown evenly.
Add the beer, pepper, rosemary, bay leaves,
sage, and continue to cook until the beer has
evaporated and a nice tasty sauce has formed.

Pay attention to the choice of the type of beer, not to make the chicken bitter

218

219

HEAVEN
SENDS US
GOOD
MEAT, BUT
THE DEVIL
SENDS US
COOKS

MEATLOAF IN CRUST

INGREDIENTS
1 pound of ground beef
$^1/_2$ onion
4 eggs
2 tablespoons of grated Parmesan cheese
1 tablespoon chopped parsley
$^1/_3$ cup of bread crumbs
1 small smoked scamorza cheese, diced
6 slices of speck
10 oz of puff pastry
extra virgin olive oil, salt and pepper to taste

In a frying pan with 6-7 tablespoons of oil,
cook the thinly-sliced onion. Add the meat and
brown well. Transfer to a bowl and let cool. Add
3 beaten eggs, Parmesan cheese, bread
crumbs, salt, pepper, parsley and scamorza.
Mix all the ingredients well, and with oiled
hands, form a loaf. Roll out the pastry. Place
loaf in center of pastry, cover with speck
lengthwise. Close dough over the top and sides,
seal the ends, glaze with egg. Transfer the roll
to a baking tray lined with parchment paper or
greased with butter.
Bake in preheated oven at 400° until the crust
is golden brown (40-45 minutes).
Transfer to a bed of salad on a platter. Slice and
serve the meatloaf at the table.

223

224

To make the taste of the meatloaf sweeter, use white instead of smoked scamorza

RABBIT IN A PAN

INGREDIENTS
3 pounds of rabbit
1 clove of garlic
1 glass of red wine
1 onion
3-4 bay leaves
4 ripe tomatoes chopped parsley
extra virgin olive oil, salt and pepper to taste

Clean the rabbit and cut into pieces. Wash it with brine, and dry it. Sauté 1 clove of garlic in 7-8 tablespoons of oil. Add the rabbit. Cook it pouring in the red wine. Let it evaporate. Add the sliced onion, bay leaf, parsley, chopped tomatoes, salt and pepper. Cook over medium heat, adding, if necessary, a bit of warm water for approximately 1 hour.

SAUSAGE WITH ONION AND POTATOES

INGREDIENTS
2 pounds of sausage
4 pounds of yellow potatoes
2 medium-sized onions
5-6 bay leaves
salt and pepper to taste

In a large frying pan place the sausage in a single layer poking it with the tines of a fork. Turn occasionally. Meanwhile peel the potatoes. Cut them into pieces and soak in water and salt. When the sausage is half cooked drain the potatoes and add them to the sausage along with the bay leaf and the very thinly sliced onion. Put the lid on the pan. Continue cooking over low heat (use flame spreader), occasionally shaking pan. Transfer the well-browned sausage with potatoes to a serving dish. Serve hot with a sprinkling of black pepper.

229

SLICING ALLOWS FOR DISTRIBUTION OF FLAVOR AND QUICKER COOKING TIME

SCHIACCIATINE "ALLA PIZZAIOLA"

INGREDIENTS
1 pound of ground beef
2 tablespoons of grated Parmesan
2 tablespoons of pecorino
$^1/_2$ cup of bread crumbs
1 tablespoon of chopped parsley
1 clove of garlic
$^1/_2$ cup of flour
$^3/_4$ pound of peeled tomatoes, chopped
2 tablespoons pickled capers
1 tablespoon of oregano
extra virgin olive oil, salt and pepper to taste

In a bowl combine the meat, 1 teaspoon salt, egg, bread crumbs, cheese, parsley, and a pinch of freshly ground pepper. Mix the ingredients with your hands so that they are well-blended. Make patties. Add flour and press them between your palms so that they are nice and smooth.
In a large frying pan pour $^1/_2$ cup of olive oil. When hot, lay the patties in a single layer. Fry on both sides, and add the chopped tomatoes. Continue cooking over medium heat for quarter of an hour.
Two minutes before turning off the heat, add the capers and a sprinkle of oregano.
Serve warm.

STEP 1

STEP 2

234

STEP 3

VEAL FILLET WITH BRANDY

INGREDIENTS
1 veal fillet about 2 pounds
3-4 cloves of garlic, whole
1 beef bouillon cube
1 cup brandy or cognac
1 cup extra virgin olive oil

Pour oil in a roasting pan. Add the garlic and brown over medium heat. Lay the fillet. Fry it well on all sides and season with the crumbled bouillon cube. Pour the brandy with the heat off so that it does not ignite. Cook for 2 minutes on stovetop, then transfer to a preheated oven at 450° for about 20 minutes until the alcohol has evaporated. Let the meat cool. Then slice it thinly and place in a serving dish. Serve the tenderloin with the cooking sauce in a gravy boat.

237

STEP 1

238

STEP 2

STEP 3

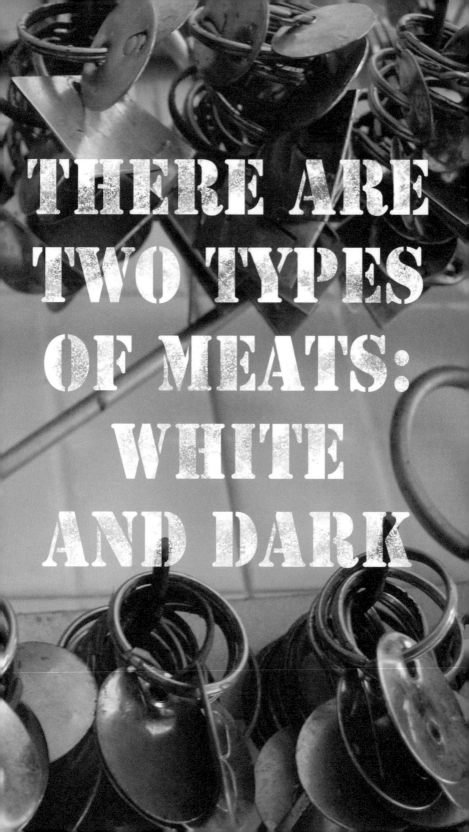

THERE ARE TWO TYPES OF MEATS: WHITE AND DARK

MEMO:

The octopus is cooked
in its own water.

fish

NEVER FRY A FISH TILL IT'S CAUGHT

BREAM BAKED IN PARCHMENT PAPER

INGREDIENTS
4 breams $^3/_4$ pound each
2 lemons
1 bunch of parsley
4 teaspoons oregano or thyme
extra virgin olive oil and salt to taste

Gut the bream. Cut the fins. Rinse, dry. Place each bream in the center of large sheet of parchment paper. Season with a pinch of salt and a sprinkling of oregano, to taste. In the abdominal cavity place a few leaves of parsley and chopped lemon. Close the parchment paper. Put them in a baking dish. Bake in a preheated oven at 350° for about half an hour. Bring the fish to the table in the parchment paper and serve with parsley and lemon juice.

247

STEP 1

STEP 2

249

STEP 3

FRESH COD FILETS
"ALL'ACQUA PAZZA"

INGREDIENTS
8 fillets of cod
2 cloves of garlic
$1/_2$ medium onion
12-15 cherry tomatoes
1 bunch of parsley
$1/_2$ cup bread crumbs
extra virgin olive oil and salt to taste

In a large pan pour 7-8 tablespoons of olive oil,
whole garlic cloves, thinly sliced onion and
cook over a low heat for 2-3 minutes. Add the
tomatoes, cut in half, the chopped parsley, and
4-5 tablespoons of water.
After 2 minutes, lay in the cod fillets. Cover
them with a bit of water. Cover the pan and
cook over low heat without turning the fish.
Towards the end, add salt.
With the aid of a spatula remove the cod fillets,
and place them on a serving dish keeping them
as warm as possible.
In the pan with the sauce sprinkle the bread
crumbs. Raise the heat so that it browns. Pour
the sauce over the fish and serve.

251

253

FRIED SHRIMP AND SQUID

INGREDIENTS
1 pound of prawns
1 pound of squid
6 tablespoons of flour
1 lemon
extra virgin olive oil and salt to taste

Shell and devein the shrimps. Wash, dry and flour them.
Clean the squid. Remove the tentacles, and leave them whole. Cut the main body into strips crosswise, creating rings of squid. Wash, dry, flour, and shake them a little to remove excess flour.
In a pan with hot oil, fry the shrimp first, then the squid. Take care to cover the container with a lid to avoid the hot splatter.
When both are golden brown, drain them on paper towels using a slotted spoon. Sprinkle with salt. Transfer to a serving dish and serve together very hot with lemon cut into wedges.

255

THE SHORE IS GEOLOGICALLY MODIFIED BY THE ACTION OF THE BODY OF WATER PAST AND PRESENT

SALAD WITH TUNA

INGREDIENTS
7 oz tuna chunks
7 oz cherry tomatoes
1 oz capers
extra virgin olive oil
salt

Drain the water from the canned tuna. Cut the cherry tomatoes in half and mix them with the tuna, adding salt, extra virgin olive oil and capers.

You can also
add diced pickles

259

SEA BASS
ON A BED OF LEMON

INGREDIENTS
bream or sea bass (about 1 pound for each diner)
3-4 lemons
parsley
extra virgin olive oil and salt to taste

Flake, gut, wash and dry the sea bream or sea bass. In a baking dish, arrange lemon slices to form a bed, and lay the oiled and salted fish on it. Bake in a preheated oven at 350° after having covered the pan with a sheet of aluminum. The time will vary from 30 to 50 minutes depending on the thickness of the fish. When ready to serve, garnish with lemon and fresh sprigs of parsley.

261

SEAFOOD SALAD

INGREDIENTS
1 medium octopus
$^2/_3$ pound cuttlefish
1 pound shrimp
4-5 lemons
1 glass of white wine vinegar
chopped parsley
extra virgin olive oil, salt and pepper to taste

Clean and wash the octopus and cuttlefish
(remove the ink bags), cut the bags into strips
and the tentacles into pieces; in a pot with
water and 1 glass of vinegar, boil the octopus,
adding salt; follow the same procedure for the
cuttlefish in a separate pan.

Shell the shrimps and cook them for 5 minutes
in a bit of water; drain them and let them cool.
In a serving dish, place the well-drained
octopus and cuttlefish, add the shrimps,
season with olive oil, parsley, lemon juice, salt
and pepper, mix well and leave to cool and
season. Serve at least one hour after
preparation.

263

STEAMED OCTOPUS

INGREDIENTS
2 $1/4$ pounds octopus
2 celery heart
1 yellow carrot
1 onion
2 cloves of garlic
1 bunch of parsley
10-15 black peppercorns
$1/2$ cup white wine
4 bay leaves
2 cups tomato sauce
extra virgin olive oil and salt to taste

Clean the octopus and cut it into pieces if large
(leave them whole if the octopuses are small
enough). Put it in a pot with a clove of garlic,
bay leaves, a dash of white wine and let it cook
for an hour or so in its own water at low heat.
At this point, transfer it to a terracotta pot, add
a half cup of olive oil, sliced onion, a clove of
garlic, chopped parsley, the celery heart,
carrot slices and peppercorns; add the tomato
sauce and a pinch of salt; bring it to boil in a
covered pot.

265

SWORDFISH WITH MEDITERRANEAN SCENTS

INGREDIENTS
4 slices of swordfish with a thickness of about $^1/_2$ inch.
15-20 cherry tomatoes
2 tablespoons black olives, pitted
4 teaspoons small capers
2 sprigs of rosemary
grated rind of 2 fresh lemons
extra virgin olive oil

Prepare 4 sheets of parchment paper of the appropriate size to contain one slice of swordfish. Make each parchment paper with 1 slice of fish, 4-5 tomatoes cut in half, 5-6 olives, 1 teaspoon capers, $^1/_2$ sprig of rosemary, 1 grated lemon peel, and a sprinkling with oil. Close the parchment paper and steam for about 20 minutes.
Open the parchment paper at the table, after having served each diner.

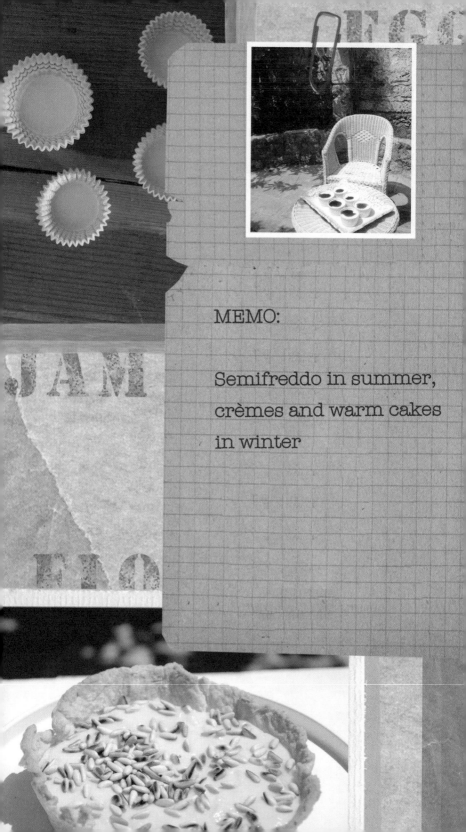

MEMO:

Semifreddo in summer,
crèmes and warm cakes
in winter

desserts

AMARETTI
WITH CREAM

INGREDIENTS
5 eggs
5 tablespoons of sugar
1 pound of mascarpone
4-5 tablespoons of rum
$\frac{1}{4}$ pound of amaretti biscuits

In a bowl, put the egg yolks with the sugar and
whisk with an electric mixer until you have
formed a light and frothy cream. Add the
mascarpone and rum stirring with a wooden
spoon. Add the crumbled amaretti biscuits and
mix well. Gently fold in the egg whites until
stiff. When the ingredients are well blended
put the cream in the freezer for 2 hours for it
to acquire smooth consistency. Then keep it in
the fridge until ready to serve. Serve with
slices of sponge cake, pan d'oro or lingue di
gatto biscuits.

When cooking the crème, stir
with a wooden spoon always
stirring in the same direction

271

CAKE
WITH APPLES
AND PINE NUTS

INGREDIENTS
10 oz of puff pastry
5-6 apples
6-7 tablespoons of brown sugar
7-8 tablespoons of pine nuts

Line a 9" round pie pan with parchment paper.
Lay the dough on the bottom and sides of the
pan. Peel the apples. Cut them first into two,
then four, then into eight wedges and take out
the seeds. Spread the apples on the pastry.
Sprinkle them with sugar and pine nuts. Cook
in a preheated oven at 180° for about half an
hour. Serve the cake warm.

STEP 3

STEP 4

STEP 5

THE APPLE
IS A SYMBOL
FOR
KNOWLEDGE
AND
IMMORTALITY

CRESCENTS
WITH JAM

INGREDIENTS
For the dough:
1 pound of flour
1 pinch of salt
1 $^3/_4$ sticks of butter
1 cup of sugar
1 small glass of dry white wine
3 eggs
zest of 1 lemon

For the filling:
$^3/_4$ pound of grape jam or other jam
1 egg
powdered sugar

280

Pour the flour onto a pastry board with a pinch of salt, sugar, and lemon zest. Mix well. Make a crater in the center, pour in the butter (melted in a double boiler) and 2 whole eggs. Knead it, combining 7-8 tablespoons of dry white wine. Work it until you get a smooth consistency. Leave it to rest for half an hour in the refrigerator.
Roll out the dough with a rolling pin to a thickness of $^3/_4$ to an inch. Cut into disks of 4 inches in diameter. Put a teaspoon of jam in the center. Brush the edges of each disk with a little beaten egg and fold it into a crescent, pressing it with your fingers to seal the edges well. Grease and flour a baking tray. Lay the cakes on it and bake it at 350° until they become golden brown. Dust with powdered sugar and serve.

281

283

FRUIT PRESERVES ARE PREPARATIONS OF FRUITS, VEGETABLES AND SUGAR, OFTEN CANNED OR SEALED FOR LONG-TERM STORAGE

DONUTS
FLAVORED
WITH ORANGE

INGREDIENTS
2 cups of flour
$^2/_3$ cup of sugar
3 eggs
1 teaspoon of baking powder
1 cup orange juice (about 5 oz)
1 cup of extra virgin olive oil
the skin of an orange, chopped very fine

In a fairly deep container pour in the eggs and
sugar. With an electric mixer, mix it lightly.
Then add the flour mixed with baking powder,
oil, orange juice and orange peel. Use the
mixer just enough to get a smooth and soft
consistency.
Pour into a greased and floured cake mold and
bake in a preheated oven at 325°
for about 30 minutes making sure to place the
pan in the oven on the top shelf. When the cake
is cooked through and golden, let it cool for five
minutes. Then take it out of the mold and serve
warm or at room temperature.

PANNA COTTA
WITH CARAMEL

INGREDIENTS
For the panna cotta:
2 cups of liquid heavy cream
1 cup whole milk
8 oz of powdered sugar
1 teaspoon of vanilla
3 sheets of gelatin

For the caramel:
8 tablespoons of brown sugar
2 tablespoons of water

Soak the sheets of gelatin in a bowl for 10 minutes. Pour the cream into a double bottom steel saucepan. Add the milk, sugar, and vanilla. Cook for about 10 minutes over a low heat, without arriving at the boiling point. Remove it from the heat. Add the well drained gelatin sheets, and continue to whisk until it is completely melted and blended with the other ingredients.

For the caramel:
Put sugar and water in a double bottom steel pan, and cook it on the flame until the sugar has melted, taking on a nice amber color. Pour the caramel into a pudding mold or individual portion mold. Twirl it so that it is spread evenly. Then pour in the panna cotta mixture. Let it cool and keep it in the refrigerator at least 1 day before serving the dessert. To remove the panna cotta more easily, soak the mold for a few seconds in hot water, place on serving dish and add a spoon of caramel on top.

289

PINOLATA

INGREDIENTS
$3/4$ pound of pastry
7-8 tablespoons of pine nuts, lightly toasted
1 pound beans (any)

For the custard:
2 cups of milk
5 tablespoons of sugar
4 tablespoons of flour
the yolks of 3 eggs
zest of 1 lemon
$3/4$ cup of pine nuts, lightly toasted

For the custard:
Whip the egg yolks and sugar with a wooden
spoon, working them until they make bubbles.
Stir in the flour, and then slowly, the warm
milk. Flavor it with the peel of a thinly sliced
lemon. Cook over moderate heat. Stir with a
wooden spoon, always in the same direction,
until the cream thickens and is smooth and
silky.
Line a buttered and floured cake tin with the
pastry. Put it on a baking sheet. Cover with
beans and bake in a preheated oven at 350° for
about 40 minutes.
When the pie is cooked and golden, remove
from oven. Remove baking paper and beans
and transfer to a serving dish. Pour in the
cream and sprinkle with pine nuts, lightly
toasted.

291

STEP

294

STEP 2

STEP 3

STEP 4

STEP 5

RASPBERRY JAM TART WITH ICE CREAM

INGREDIENTS
2 cups of sifted flour
$1^1/_4$ sticks of butter
3 tablespoons of ice cold water
10 oz of raspberry jam
vanilla ice cream

Put the flour and the butter cut into cubes in a
large bowl. Work with your fingers in order to
obtain a compound similar to bread crumbs.
Add the water a little at a time, and continue to
knead it until the dough is smooth. Form a ball,
and cover it with plastic wrap. Keep it in the
refrigerator for 2 hours.
Roll out the dough onto a sheet, and line the
bottom and sides of a buttered and floured
baking sheet. Prick with a fork in several
places. Bake in a preheated oven at 350° for 10
minutes.
Remove the crust from the oven. Cover it with
jam and let it cook, covered with aluminum foil
for 20 minutes. Cool the tart. Place on a
serving dish and serve with vanilla ice cream.

297

SEMIFREDDO WITH CHOCOLATE AND HAZELNUTS

INGREDIENTS
$^2/_3$ cup of unsweetened cocoa powder
8 tablespoons of sugar
2 tablespoons of flour
2 cups of milk
$^1/_3$ cup of toasted hazelnuts

In a saucepan pour the cocoa, sugar, and sifted
flour. Stir constantly with a wooden spoon.
Pour the hot milk on top. Bring it to a boil and
cook the cream over low heat for three minutes
so that it thickens.
On the bottom of a 9" round or 6" square
ceramic or glass dish, spread a cup of toasted
and crushed hazelnuts. Add the cream.
Garnish with whole hazelnuts on top. Allow it
to cool and keep it in the refrigerator 4-5 hours
before serving.

TIRAMISU'

INGREDIENTS
5 fresh eggs
5 heaping tablespoons of sugar
1 pound mascarpone
2 tablespoons of rum
$^3/_4$ pound of biscuits, ladyfingers or pavesini type
6-7 tablespoons of espresso
3-4 tablespoons of unsweetened cocoa powder

In a bowl beat the egg yolks and the sugar with a wooden spoon. When they bubble, stir in the mascarpone, rum. Beat the egg whites first until stiff and then fold in gently.

302 In a rectangular baking dish place a bed of biscuits. Wet them with coffee. Pour the mascarpone cream over the biscuits and sprinkle it with cocoa. Keep the tiramisù in the refrigerator for at least 3 hours before serving.

STEP 2

STEP 3

STEP 4

STEP 5

ZUCCOTTO

2 cups of ricotta cheese
3 tablespoons of sugar
$2/_3$ pound of candied fruits in small cubes
raisins
pine nuts
7 oz dark chocolate
ladyfingers to taste
$3/_4$ cup of whipped cream
2 tablespoons of marsala

Cover a zuccotto mold completely with plastic wrap, with no gaps, with ladyfingers soaked in marsala. Mix the ricotta with the sugar, add the candied fruit, raisins, pine nuts, dark chocolate in small pieces, and crumbled ladyfingers. Finally, gently add the whipped cream. Fill the mold with the mixture and finish with a layer of ladyfingers soaked in marsala. Cover with plastic wrap and store in the refrigerator for a few hours. Serve it after removing it from the mold on a serving dish.

307

There is
no recipe
you cannot
do, if you
focus on
what's
in front
of you!

Alphabetical index – by chapter

Alphabetical index – general

My recipes

My notes

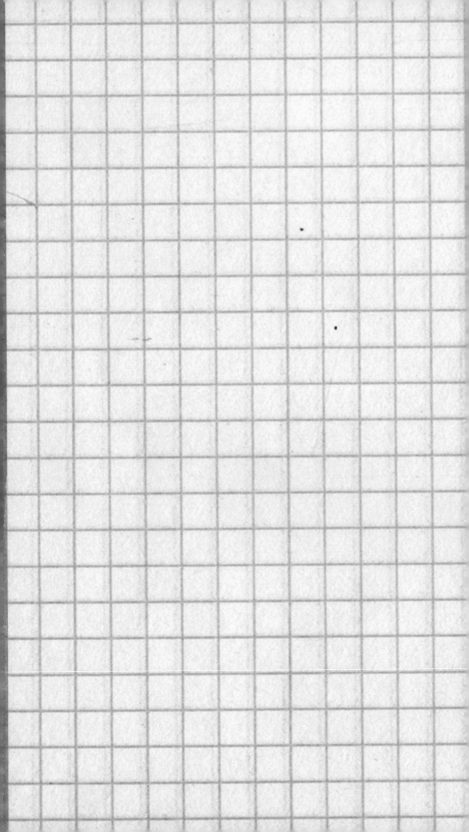

www.congedoeditore.it
© Congedo Publishing February 2014 - Galatina (Le) - Milano - Italy
ISBN 9788896483176
Printed in China

Photos by Wendy Arm
Photos by Walter e Laura Leonardi pp. 10-11, 70-71, 99, 152-153 (figs),
189, 220-221, 259, 263, 299
Photos by Francesca Meleleo pp. 78-79, 86 (baskets), 130-131
Photos by Aldo Summa pp. 8 (basil), 152-153 (cheeses), 267

Translations by: Triboo Digitale S.r.l.

Revised by: Cynthia Conigliaro